# THE CHANGING

# *North Oxford*

## BOOK TWO

# Ann Spokes Symonds

Robert Boyd
PUBLICATIONS

Published by
*Robert Boyd Publications*
260 Colwell Drive
Witney, Oxfordshire OX8 7LW

First published 1998

Copyright © Ann Spokes Symonds and
*Robert Boyd Publications*

Ann Spokes Symonds has asserted her right
to be identified as the author of this work

ISBN: 1 899536 33 7

## OTHER TITLES IN THE *CHANGING FACES* SERIES

Banbury: Book One
Bicester: Book One
Bladon with Church Hanborough and
    Long Hanborough
Botley and North Hinksey
Cowley
Cowley: Book Two
Cowley Works: Book One
Cumnor and Appleton with Farmoor
    and Eaton
St Clements and East Oxford:
    Book One
St Clements and East Oxford:
    Book Two
Eynsham: Book One
Eynsham: Book Two
Headington: Book One
Headington: Book Two
Jericho: Book One
Littlemore and Sandford
Marston: Book One
Marston: Book Two
North Oxford: Book One

Oxford City Centre: Book One
South Oxford: Book One
Summertown and Cutteslowe
St Ebbes and St Thomas: Book One
St Ebbes and St Thomas: Book Two
West Oxford
Witney: Book One
Wolvercote with Wytham and Godstow
Woodstock: Book One
Woodstock: Book Two

### FORTHCOMING
Abingdon
Banbury: Book Two
Bicester: Book Two
Chipping Norton
Cowley: Book Three
Faringdon and District
Grimsbury
Jericho: Book Two
Kennington
Thame
Yarnton and Begbroke with Cassington

Printed and bound in Great Britain at The Alden Press, Oxford

# Contents

**Cover illustrations**

Front:   The Radcliffe Observatory, 1998.

Back:   Map of Walton Manor.

# Acknowledgements

This book could not have been writtten without the help of the many people who live in or have connections with Walton Manor. Those who kindly lent me photographs are acknowledged in the text but there are others who provided me with essential information or advised me in various ways. They include:

Miss Pauline Adams, Archivist, Somerville College; Sister Anthony, Mr John Ashdown, Mrs Joan Bates, Father Jerome Bertram, Dr Elizabeth Boardman, Mr Ken Bryan, Sister Anne Burke, Mr Ron Busby, Mrs Susan Clear, Lady Colvin, Mr Chris Couch, Dr Robin Darwall-Smith, Archivist, University College; Mrs Jan Dean, Green College; Sister Patricia Devany, Dr J.A. Dodd, Mrs Molly Eagle, Mr Rob Ellis, Mrs Polly Friedhoff, St Antony's College; Mr Malcolm Graham, Mrs Audrey Harris, Mr Colin Harris, Dr D. Hopwood, Miss M. Hutchinson, Mr Bob Jefferies, Professor Michael Kaser, Mrs Martha Kempson, Mr Ray King, Mrs Deborah Kirkwood, Sister Margherita, Sister Marie Hélène, Ms Taube Marks, Dr Ross McKibbin, Acting Archivist, St John's College; Miss Paulette Micklewood, Ms Rebecca Mobey, Mrs Erica Oakes, Mrs Peacocke, Mrs Phelps, Mrs Maire Pickett, Mr Richard Pineo, Miss Joyce Pollard, Mrs A. Rees, Librarian, Dept. for Continuing Education, Oxford University; Mrs Peggy Rees, Dr Marjorie Reeves, CBE, Mrs Ann Robinson, St Antony's College, Mrs Catherine Robinson, Dr and Mrs Robb-Smith, The Reverend Max Saint, Mrs Nesta Selwyn, Dr David Smith, Librarian, St Anne's College; Mr and Mrs M. Soden, Mr Peter Strong, Ms Rachel Stuart, Mrs Joan Templeton, Mrs Valerie Thompson, Miss Stella Welford, Miss Phyllis White, Miss Kathleen White, Sir Geoffrey Wilson, Mrs Eileen Wright.

I should also like to thank my husband, Richard Symonds, for perusing my draft text and for all his help and support, Dr Desmond Walshaw for his indispensable computer skills and Dr Milo Shott for his help and advice in connection with my photographs.

I have been unable to trace the copyright holders of two pictures and anyone claiming copyright should please get in touch with me.

*Ann Spokes Symonds*

## NOTE ON THE PHOTOGRAPHS

Some of the original photographs were faded or unsharp and did not reproduce well but I have included a few for historical reasons or to illustrate a point. I hope that readers will therefore forgive the quality in order that they can at least gain an impression and be able to appreciate the atmosphere of the place, people or event.

# *Introduction*

The roots of Walton go deeper down in time than those of Norham and the social mix is more diverse.

When the foundations of buildings were being dug in Polstead Road and Kingston Road some implements and arrowheads dating from Roman times were found and in the days when Oxford was no more than a small Saxon settlement there were people living in Walton.

Its earliest Lord of the Manor, according to the Domesday Survey, was Roger D'Ivri in 1086. At this time there were various spellings: Wattone and Waltona as well as Walton. The name is Saxon and means the tun by the wall (i.e. the City wall), a tun being an enclosed piece of land or homestead. Antony Wood, the 17th century local historian and antiquary, thought the name was derived from ' Waldune', a dune signifying a hill or mound standing on a rise in a large valley (like Beaumont). Wood not only refers to the gravel pits and wells in the area but also to stones 'cut with great cunning . . . all carrying with them convincing signs of some eminent place formerly there.' Gravel was dug in Walton since at least the 16th century.

Some portion of the land seems to have been given to Roger D'Oily by William the Conqueror who was described by Ingram (in his 1837 *Memorials*) as 'the sworn brother and fellow adventurer of Roger D'Ivri.' Ingram goes on to point out that as these Norman chiefs seem to have experienced some difficulty retaining their newly acquired territory, the land 'fell promptly into the occupation of Brumman the Rich who already owned land, including 24 acres of meadow, at a place called Brumman's well.' It is assumed that this well was the one which was later called Walton well.

People often ask where the manor house was situated but although there was a manor farm (where Lucy's iron foundry is situated) there seems to be no record of a manor house. This may be because the owners of the land through the years had their own large houses or manors elsewhere.

In the 12th century Walton was owned by St George's Church in Oxford Castle and then by Oseney Abbey. The physician to King Henry VIII, George Owen of Godstow, was Lord of the manor when it consisted of four houses, three cottages, some arable land and a fishery. His son Richard sold Walton Manor to St John's College in 1573. It was not to be developed for housing until nearly three centuries later.

Although, as in Norham Manor, most of the land was owned by St John's College, here they not only sold off plots for large family houses but built homes for their own college servants and artisans. Consequently, unlike Norham society it was not dominated by the University academics and therefore there was less snobbery.

Also, as in Norham Manor, most of the roads were named after St John's livings: Chalfont, Farndon, Frenchay, Kingston, Leckford, Longworth, Polstead, Southmoor, Tackley and Warnborough.

In 1954, Lionel Brett, the architect, was retained by St John's College to prepare a development plan for much of the Walton Manor area to the west of Woodstock Road. Described as a fairly extensive 'Master plan', it included flats, shops and refurbishment. It was also to have new roads to the cost of which the City Council was to be asked to contribute. However, it was never fully carried out. Even so, it remained an important part of the college's strategy for their Walton Manor houses.

In 1967 Lord Esher (as Brett had become on the death of his father in 1963) was quoted in *The Times* of 3rd January: 'Like the mews and cottage dwellings of central London its [Walton Manor's] small houses now have a wider appeal and there is no reason why its present domestic scale should not be retained indefinitely'. This suggests that 13 years on from the more drastic 1954 scheme the area was now being looked at in terms of conservation. In any case, after the Leasehold Reform Act of that year so many people qualified to buy their leases in various parts of the estate that wholesale development was not feasible.

Houses of a pleasant domestic scale typical of the Walton Manor estate. The variegated brick work can be seen on many of the early 19th century dwellings.

Today, Walton Manor, which is a Conservation Area, could be described as individualistic, heightened by its variety and with a healthy mixture of town and gown.

# *The Outward Face of Walton Manor*

Numbers 28 and 30 Plantation Road before restoration. A bakery was once situated here the entrance to which was in the street beyond the wall. The house is now No. 30. As the name of the road indicates, there was once a plantation here. It was on the site of Tagg's Garden, the Tagg family having for years been in the nursery garden business, holding various pieces of land on the outskirts of Oxford. By the time of the 1832 Enclosure Award it had already been laid out as building plots.

The houses are of a smaller scale than those to the north and east. A few houses, including No. 75 had been completed even before 1832. Number 73 was built in 1850.

The road had originally been two separate lanes and gave access to Cabbage Hill which lay between Kingston and Woodstock Roads. The two parts of the road met in 1830. A map of 1850 shows Plantation Road with plantations still laid out to the north. Immediately north of Tagg's Garden was Lark Hill. In 1874 St John's College sold the gravel here to the railway company for £800. Lark Hill was once considered as a site for a Cemetery and for a Workhouse. (The above photograph and the one following courtesy of Mrs Jeannine Alton.)

Plantation Road in about the early 1950s with the Bakery seen on the right. Older residents remember the delightful smell of the newly baked bread wafting down the road. Mrs Sarah Hall at one time sold both pork pies and dough cakes from this Bakery.

The front of 30 Plantation Road, the home of Mr and Mrs Alton as it is today (February 1998) with Mrs Jeannine Alton at her front door. The Altons are very proud of the plaque on the house which was awarded them by the Oxford Preservation Trust for their careful restoration in 1977.

Plantation Road looking west in 1998 taken from the top floor of No. 30, courtesy of Mr and Mrs Alton. In the distance are the Gardeners' Arms and Wyndham House.

Plantation Road looking east towards Woodstock Road; No. 81 to the end.

Houses in Adelaide Street built in the 1830s and 1840s and thus pre-dating the development of North Oxford by St John's College. Note the pattern of the brickwork, very typical of the period.

Number 20 Adelaide Street in the foreground. It is one of the few houses in the street which is not one of a pair. It is thought that the house next door (to the west) was demolished and replaced by a wood yard.

At one time the cellar of No. 20 was a mortuary and the coffins were slid down a shoot (now attractively decorated with shells).

The present owner of 20 Adelaide Street, Mrs Betty Donaldson, seen here in 1998, has converted the cellar into her study.

Original railings can be seen in the front of some houses in St Bernard's Road. This is No. 7, taken in 1998. The road was first developed in 1832 and was known first as Horse and Jockey Lane. Later, it became St John's Road but because it was continually confused with St John Street, further south, the College was asked for another name in 1960. St Bernard's College was the foundation prior to that of St John the Baptist on the latter's present site.

The road is affected by the number of gravel pits which used to be scattered about the area and several houses have required major repairs over the years. At one time the houses in St Bernard's Road had privies in the gardens, sometimes some distance from the house. Those built on the north side were reached by a flight of steps because the ground slopes steeply from north to south. It must have been a difficult walk in the dark. It was only in 1993 that the last garden privy was replaced by an indoor lavatory. Another example of the difference in levels is the fact that No. 55, at the west end of the road, once the home of Mr Huggins, the butcher in North Parade, is 6 feet above the level of the Victoria pub (see Section 6) on the corner of Walton Street.

Hurst, the Oxford local historian, wrote in 1899: 'A pedestrian going there 30 years earlier would have found himself on the edge of a cliff of gravel with a row of white poplars skirting the lane, crooked and rough but one deserving to be recorded as that by which Charles I and his cavaliers with his 6,000 troops escaped from Oxford on 3rd June 1644.'

Observatory Street, south side (above and left). The stuccoed terrace houses look particularly attractive with their freshly colour-washed frontages. The street was developed from 1834 and C.J. Day explains in *The Victoria History of the County of Oxford,* Vol.IV (The City of Oxford) that the development in this street and

St Bernard's Road was a 'response to the City's growing population ... Oxford was unusual in that the movement outwards was by the less well off, leaving a ring of suburbs around an upper-class centre.' Observatory Street, north side, (right) July 1998. The road is named after the Radcliffe Observatory, situated to the south.

Numbers 121 (above) and 123 Woodstock Road, built in 1856 (photographs taken in 1997) which S.L. Seckham, the architect of Park Town, designed in the style of the houses there. However, he seemed to lose interest and William Wilkinson took over as architect in the 1860s.

The west side of the Woodstock Road opposite the Church of St Philip and St James was the centre of the projected Walton Manor Estate for St John's College and Seckham started to build here in 1856/60. Woodstock Road, which runs south to north through the area, was once turnpiked and when the road was first built it had a trench on its west side. Scrapings from the road, which once consisted of horse manure and excavations from house cellars, were thrown into the ditch and this is the reason why so many healthy trees grew at the side of the road.

Numbers 91–95 Woodstock Road which are 19th century Grade II listed buildings of special architectural and historic interest.

The Shrubbery, 72 Woodstock Road which is now the home of the Principal of St Hugh's College. This is a view from the west taken in 1997. It was built in about 1850 and is listed of special architectural and historic interest because it contains a fine plaster ceiling of 1571 which, with a frieze of vine leaves and mermaids, came originally from the building on the corner of Cornmarket and High Street which was demolished in 1900. Thomas Mallam, owner of No. 72, had a new room built on to the house in order to take the Tudor ceiling.

The Shrubbery from the south (1998). Tanys Hinchcliffe in her important book on North Oxford (Yale University Press, 1992) explains how the house came into being: 'Some of the most active businessmen of Oxford had already begun to regard North Oxford as a middle-class place of residence by building substantial houses on land they had scraped together from owners other than the college [St John's]'. It was thus that Thomas Mallam, who was first a tobacconist and then an auctioneer, came to build The Shrubbery. He was Mayor in 1847. The house, nick-named 'Quidville', therefore preceded the great development of the area by St. John's. The house was once the home of the Maison Française before it moved to Norham Road in 1963.

Sir George and Lady Whitehead in 1930 when they lived at The Shrubbery. Standing, left to right: Mercy (later Mrs Nankivell), Lady Whitehead, Joan. Seated: Peter de Putron, Mary Russell Vick (née de Putron) who later played hockey for England, Sir George Whitehead holding John de Putron. Peter, Mary and John were grandchildren. The Whiteheads lived at the Shrubbery from 1920 to 1943. (Photograph courtesy of Mrs Susan Clear.)

Peter de Putron watering plants in the garden of The Shrubbery in 1930. Number 74 Woodstock Road, to the north, was by Wilkinson and Moore. (Photograph courtesy of Mrs Susan Clear.)

113 Woodstock Road, designed by William Wilkinson, one of the illustrations in his book *English Country Houses* (1875). It is entitled 'House in Walton Manor: Oxford'. Wilkinson, one of the most distinguished and prolific architects of his day, was an exponent of the Gothic. He was soon joined by his nephew, Harry Wilkinson Moore, who was as prolific as his uncle. Their buildings are mainly Gothic in red or yellow brick with stone facings. They designed houses directly for a purchaser's own home or on behalf of property speculators who were active in North Oxford at the time. By 1867 Wilkinson was responsible for approving all the suburb's building proposals. H.W. Moore later became an emulator of the architect Thomas Graham Jackson's English Rennaissance style. Number 113 was built in 1863 for Edwin Butler, wine merchant.

Butler Close. The flats were built on the site of No. 113, on the corner of Leckford Road. It was named after the owner of the original house and also after Miss C. Violet Butler, a well-known pioneer in the field of social and community work, who lived in North Oxford. (Photograph taken in 1997).

Number 68 Woodstock Road which was originally the Vicarage of St Philip and St James. It is now the Middle East Centre, St Antony's College. (Photograph taken in April 1998.

The front part of the hall at 68 Woodstock Road. Nikolaus Pevsner and Jennifer Sherwood in their *Buildings of England. Oxfordshire* describe it as a 'cumbersome half-timbered and tile-hung house by H.G.W. Drinkwater, 1886/7.' The Rev. Bill Vervon thought that the house was a 'draughty old barn' and was thrilled to move to a newly built Vicarage in the grounds of the old house in 1956. The former Vicarage was then bought by St Antony's College and became the home of Professor Kenneth Kirkwood, his wife Deborah and their six children who lived there from 1956 to 1975. He was Rhodes Professor of Race Relations. They settled happily in there. Before that they had been in accommodation on the two top floors at 4 Church Walk which could only be approached by an outside fire escape and the kitchen was on the fourth floor. It had not been easy for them there with six children and where only their two au pairs had their own bedrooms.

The back part of the hall at 68 Woodstock Road. The panelling was brought from a former country house. Changes were made to the house in 1975 when the Kirkwoods moved out.

The dining-room at 68 Woodstock Road during the Kirkwood's time. The old refrectory table was originally at Wytham Abbey.

The Master bedroom in the old Vicarage during the time the Kirkwood's lived there. The bed is made from pieces of old panelling bought in St Clement's. (All the above four photographs by Mr Anthony Kirkwood, courtesy of Mrs. D. Kirkwood.)

The Director of the Middle East Centre, Dr. Derek Hopwood OBE, Faculty Fellow of St Antony's College and University Reader in Modern Middle Eastern Studies, in the Library of 68 Woodstock Road. Part of the old hall is now incorporated in the Library.

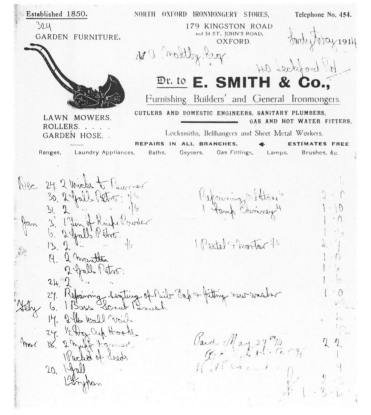

A 1914 bill sent to a resident in Leckford Road by E. Smith & Co., North Oxford Ironmongery Stores. Note the written list which includes wicks, petrol, a scrubbing brush, hooks, nails, muff warmers and a packet of seeds. The printed heading includes the words Locksmiths, Bellhangers and Sheet Metal Workers. Here people could buy everything they needed in the hardware line including paraffin and oil lamps. The locksmith business later moved further south into Walton Street, remaining there until 1998.

The bells hung by Smith's were not church bells but bells in people's homes for ringing to summon domestic staff. The photograph (taken by courtesy of Mrs M. Pinsent) shows a row of bells typical of those of the period which were situated in the basement or ground floor kitchen; the bells were usually identified by room names or numbers.

Kingston Road looking north in the 1920s. On the corner, left, is Blanchard's (or Blachard's) which sold popular cream cakes and lardy cakes. On the right, now Partymania, were Smith's the Ironmongers; part of the lettering can be seen here. Note the tram lines in the road. The trams came from town via Beaumont Steet and the terminus was on the corner of Leckford Road.

Kingston Road looking north in 1998. Partymania, 179 Kingston Road, which has replaced Smith's the ironmongers. It sells every conceivable article one needs in order to throw a party.

Numbers 176, 177 and 178 Kingston Road, east side, south end, taken in 1998. Note the typical variegated brickwork. The road did not exist in the 1860s when there were acres of gardens and the lane called Cabbage Hill curved round through them.

Terraces of artisans' houses in Kingston Road designed by C.C. Rolfe in 1870 and now listed grade II. The blocks comprise (from south to north) numbers 159–164 and 119–128. Built for clerks, small shopkeepers and artisans, many are now inhabited by University families. In the early days quite a few were let out by their owners. Robert Hill, for instance, leased Nos. 114–119. Francis Tuck, chemist, probably leased and let out Nos. 145–147 and Thomas Walker, describing himself as a Gent's servant, let out Nos. 149–156. Earliest inhabitants included 3 spinsters, 3 widows, 3 stationers, 2 masons, 2 college servants, a tailor, 2 'gentlemen', 1 builder, 2 carpenters, a boat builder, a cabinet maker and a dairyman. One of these end-of-terrace houses was advertised for sale in April 1998 for £250,000.

Hayfield Road looking north in 1998.

Houses in Hayfield Road in 1998. The road was much used at one time by traffic avoiding the Woodstock Road but is now closed to vehicles at the southern end. All the houses in the road were designed by H.W. Moore and at least half were built by Kingerlee's. They were intended as working men's cottages and kept small at the request of St John's College.

Celebratory dancing in Hayfield Road on the occasion of its centenary in 1985.

Four ladies who were all born in Hayfield Road taken on the day of the Centenary Party in 1985. Left to right: Alice Gibbs (née Johnson) whose parents ran the dairy and ice cream parlour at No. 49. Doris Thicke (née Slade) who during World War II worked at the munitions factory at Lucy's, Evelyn Kirkland (née Harris) descended from Arthur Harris, landlord of the Anchor (see Section 6) in the 1840s, Nora Surman, (née Giles) daughter of Charlie Giles, a notable character, who was an Inspector with the Great Western Railway. He was once reported for swearing at the Duke of Marlborough but it was said that the Duke swore at him first. [For further information see: *Hayfield Road. 900 years of an Oxford Neighbourhood,* by Catherine Robinson and Elspeth Buxton, 1993, currently available from Bunters in Hayfield Road.]

Walton Well. The drinking fountain in Walton Well Road, designed by H.W. Moore, was erected in 1885 by William Ward, coal merchant. It was said that he hoped the supply of water to drink would counteract the large number of pubs in the area. From the earliest times of Walton Manor there was a well on this site. There was also a gravel pit nearby. Aristotle's Well was further north, about opposite the Anchor Inn.

Houses in Walton Well Road. Longworth Road is on the left. Here early leaseholders in houses built between 1887 and 1890 included the wife of an engine driver, a carpenter and a college cook.

Walton Well Road, north side. To the left in the photograph (taken in 1998) is the way to Port Meadow and to the recent Waterside development.

Number 2 Walton Well Road, the house of the Ironmaster of the adjacent Lucy's foundry. He had it built on an angle so that he could see in three directions, perhaps so that he could watch the comings and goings of those who worked in the foundry. The house later became the Catholic Workers' College which was founded in 1921 as a memorial to Father Charles Plater, Secretary of the Catholic Social Guild, who had died that year. It had opened with three students in two rooms but later transferred to this house. The University gave the students permission to attend lectures and to take certain diploma examinations. In 1955 the College, known by then as Plater College, moved to Boar's Hill. It is now in Pullen's Lane, Headington.

The building here at 2 Walton Well Road then became Lucy's Social Club. Because of its name it was once mistaken for something else by a visiting French scholar who had thought it might be of use in connection with his research on Chinese eroticsm. The house is now an Estate Agent's.

Numbers 12 and 13 (left) Tackley Place (taken in February 1998) both built in 1877. Dr William Brewster left St John's College £2,000 in 1725 with which to buy the advowson of Tackley after which college living the road was named.

Houses on the east side of Southmoor Road taken in April 1998. The road celebrated its centenary on 22nd June 1986 when a street party was held. The houses were built between 1882 and 1887 when the first leaseholders came in. They included shopkeepers, craftsmen, builders, spinsters and widows. As in Kingston Road, many bought up several houses and presumably let them out to others. The College originally intended the road to be of cottages and were disappointed when they saw how large the houses were and how they could be leased out at high rents. They felt that there was a need for cottage properties.

Southmoor Road houses. Note the ironwork in front and the attractive oval doorways. The majority of the houses in the road are the work of Wilkinson and Moore although 28 of them were built without the services of an architect. About 19 different builders were involved. Photograph taken in April 1998.

Houses on the north side of Farndon Road. From the left are Nos. 21 and 22 and then 23 and 24. On the right are 25 and 26. All were built by John Money to the designs of Wilkinson and Moore. (Nos. 25 and 26 just by Wilkinson.) Although semi-detached, the houses were built on a larger scale than those in many of the roads to the south because they were further enough away from the canal and railway and thus thought to appeal to a clientele higher up the social scale. In 1851 the road had earlier been considered as a site for a large railway station for the London, Oxford, Worcester and Wolverhampton line but it was never proceeded with and thus Farndon Road was able to be developed free of any threat to its sobriety in the 1870s and 1880s.

Numbers 18 and 19 Farndon Road were also built by John Money and designed by Wilkinson and Moore. Money built many houses including some in Frenchay, Polstead and St Margaret's Roads. Walter Gray, known as the Father of Oxford Conservatism, and one-time Mayor of Oxford, had come to the City as a young man to take up the post of Steward at Keble College. He later became an auctioneer and estate agent and was a friend and business partner of John Money. In fact, before their relationship Money was said to have had little reputation of substance. Gray's son (later an M.P.) gave an account of how the two men worked: 'My father would pick up from the floor a roll of plans, which he would pitch across the room to be caught by John Money. "I got these plans from St John's today, what do you think it would cost to build a house like that?" John Money would look at the plans for about five minutes and say "I should think about £2,000." to which Walter would reply: "Well, you had better get on with it John."' It was all trust between them and no contracts were exchanged. Money was the leaseholder of No. 25 Farndon Road.

From 1st January 1883, married women were allowed to hold property separately from their husbands. One of the first was Elizabeth Hurst and Walter Gray arranged for her to take the leases of 23 and 24 Farndon Road because the money was her own and free from the control of her husband.

No. 67 (left) and 69 Chalfont Road in 1998. The architect was H.W. Moore who was responsible for all the houses in the road except the odd numbers 1–7. They were built between 1892 and 1899. Of the total of about 60 original leaseholders in the road, nine were described as spinsters and seven as widows.

The backs of the houses on the east side of Chalfont Road taken from Polstead Road in 1998. Note the extensive gardens.

Numbers (left to right) 14, 16 and 18 Frenchay Road, July 1988. The architect was H.W. Moore and the builder Money (as were 22—42 and 13—23). The first leaseholder of No. 14 was W.F. Buckell, Auctioneer, and Nos. 16 and 18 were leased by Edward Giles, draper.

Polstead Road taken in the early years of the 20th century (copywright Jeremy's Postcards, Oxford Stamp Centre). All the houses were designed by H.W. Moore and erected by various builders including Hutchins, Castle and Martin, Hastings and Money. The trees have now grown to a great height.

Belsyre Court on the corner of Observatory Street and Woodstock Road, taken in 1997. It was the first large block of flats in Oxford, built in 1936 to the designs of Ernest R. Barrow and it also included offices and shops. A little row of unpretentious shops on the Woodstock Road frontage, with people living above, which once bore the name South Parade, was pulled down for the development. It also replaced the Plume and Feathers (see Section 6). St Giles Brewery was also on the site for about 90 years from 1832. In 1932 the land had been thought suitable for a theatre.

The flats from Observatory Street, taken in 1997. The Inland Revenue Office was housed in Belsyre Court from 1936 until the early 1990s ago. The blocks of flats were intended to be much more extensive and a greater number of the houses in St Bernard's Road (then St John Street) might have been demolished for that purpose. However, the builders were not able to make the ground settle despite drilling holes and filling them with tons of tar. The difficulty was caused by the gravel pits which were once situated here. There are some missing numbers (no even ones) which lend credence to this. Gravel had been extracted from this area since at least the 16th century and the place is pitted with holes.

The Alexandra Club on the northern corner of Farndon Road is run by the YWCA.
Opened by Princess Alexandra in 1971, it houses 103 residents, young women who are
studying or working in Oxford. It aims to provide affordable, secure accommodation.

# *Colleges and Schools*

## Somerville

The main entrance of Somerville in Woodstock Road. Founded in 1879, it was named for the distinguished scientist Mary Somerville (1780–1872). In its early days Somerville Hall (its then name) was in Walton House which lay between Woodstock Road and Walton Street. It was built by Alderman Thomas Ensworth in about 1826. Before Somerville took it over it was the home of Charles Mostyn Owen, Chief Constable of Oxfordshire.

Darbishire Quad in August 1997. This was named after Helen Darbishire who was Principal from 1931 to 1945. She was the daughter of an Oxford doctor and educated at Oxford High School. Somerville has always had a reputation for academic success and in the 1920s and 1930s was often called the 'blue-stocking' college. Many of its graduates have also been successful and distinguished public servants and it has produced two Prime Ministers — Margaret Thatcher and Indira Gandhi — several M.P.s, including Eleanor Rathbone and Shirley Williams, and at least six life peers. Writers of note such as Dorothy Sayers, whose *Gaudy Night* is assumed to be set in Somerville, and Iris Murdoch were also at the college. Keble, a former all-men's college, now has a Somervillian, Dr Averil Cameron, as head.

In the mid-1960s the Vaughan building, named after Dame Janet Vaughan, and the Wolfson building were erected and in more recent years the Dorothy Hodgkin building incorporating the Margaret Thatcher centre.

One of the most distinguished Somervillians was Dorothy Hodgkin (1910–1994) who is the only British woman to have won the Nobel prize, in her case for chemistry. She was a Fellow of Somerville and at one time lived at 74 Woodstock Road. Royal Mail produced this stamp in a series on well-known British women. (Copyright the Post Office, all rights reserved.)

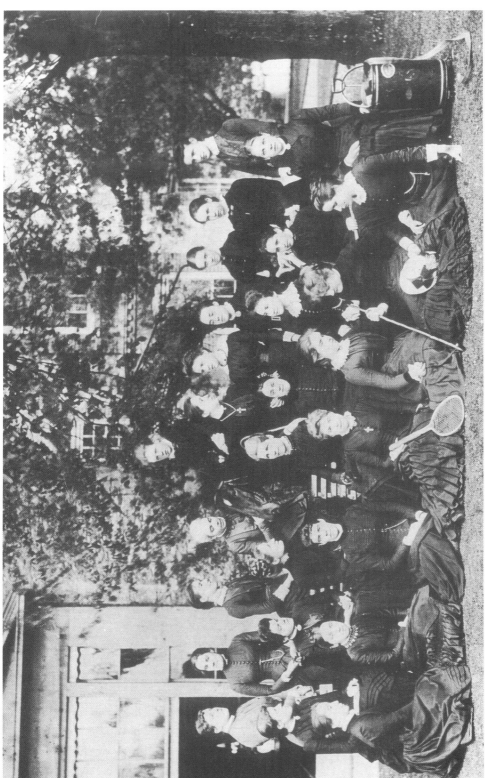

Somerville students in 1885 with their first Principal, from 1879 to 1889) Miss Madeleine Shaw Lefevre, who is seated in the centre, and some of Somerville's earliest tutors (middle row). Seated on Nobby, the horse, is Edith Coombs who was to perish in the Boxer rising in China. (Courtesy of the Principal and Fellows of Somerville College.)

A Somerville group of 1890 which includes the first Indian women to study at Oxford, Cornelia Sorabji, and the two Princesses Duleep Singh in the front row. (Courtesy of the Principal and Fellows of Somerville College.)

Somervillians say 'No' to admitting male members. Taken in the Darbishire quad in February 1992. The college's decision to become co-residential did not meet with the approval of some of the undergraduates. St Hilda's is now the only college to admit women only. (Photograph courtesy of Pauline Adams).

## St Anne's

The Association for the Education of Women in Oxford was founded in 1878 and by the following year there were 25 students who were not attached to any college but were supervised by the Association. This was the beginning of the Society of Oxford Home-Students. It was so-called because the women either lived at home or with hostesses in hostels. In 1898 the first common-room opened in 131 High Street and in 1910 it moved to 16 Ship Street where a kitchen as well as a common-room was available.

Here the members of the Home-Student clubs, such as tennis and rowing, are posing by the river in 1899. Mrs Bertha Johnson (who became the first Principal in 1893) and Mrs (T.H.) Charlotte Green are seated (in bonnets) on the bank.

By 1937 the Society was situated at Musgrave House in South Parks Road but the following year it was able to acquire houses in between the Banbury and Woodstock Roads. Here the grounds were spacious enough for a succession of buildings to be erected from 1938 onwards. Before the houses, Nos. 39 and 41, designed by Frederick Codd, were built the land was part meadow and known as Orchard's End. Both Mr G.W. Cooper of Cooper and Boffin and Mayor in 1895, and Mr James Hughes, head of the grocery firm of Grimbly Hughes, once lived at 'Witney Lodge' (No. 39). Number 41 was leased by Mr James Ryman, the Oxford print-seller, who let it to various tenants. It later became a boarding house for the Oxford High School for Girls and then a Nurses' hostel. In 1942 The Home-Students became St Anne's Society and in 1952 it finally received its charter and became St Anne's College.

The Principal and tutors of St Anne's in 1943. Back row, left to right: Olwen Rhys, Alice Huntington, The Hon Eleanor Plumer (Principal), Kirstie Morrison, Ivy Williams, Helena Deneke, Dorothy Lane-Poole, Morag Leys, Cecile Hugon. Front row: Violet Butler, Elaine Griffiths, Marjorie Reeves, Ursula Wykes. (Group photographs courtesy of St Anne's College.)

In war-time the Principal and many of the dons volunteered for war-work. Most college dons were on a register of war-work in Oxford. Their help was even needed early in the 1939/45 war on the night when the London evacuees arrived. Miss Greer, Principal of LMH, Miss Marjorie Reeves, History don at St Anne's, and Miss Lorimer, Classics don at Somerville, were summoned and taken by taxi to the old ice rink in Botley Road. After stepping over the bodies of sleeping evacuees they spent the whole night cutting, buttering and spreading jam on mountains of sandwiches. As they worked through the night they discussed the future of education in Britain. Miss Lorimer, being a very academic person, spent much of the time trying to match up the triangles of bread. (I am indebted to Dr Marjorie Reeves, CBE, for this story). The Hon Eleanor Plumer, Principal, spent the long vacations working as a munitions factory hand in Cowley where the women of the gang found her socially puzzling. Asked if she was something to do with the University she replied that she was 'just in the office' and when asked her name said 'Just call me Nell'.

St Anne's hockey team in 1946 when they were joint winners of 'Cuppers' with LMH. Back row, left to right: B. Burns, S. Peto, H. Miller, D. Sammons, R. Huggan. Front row: J. Harrison (hockey blue), M. Hodgkinson, A. Spokes (Captain), J. Perrin, M. Davies. (Absent D. Wootton.)

The dining-hall at St Anne's soon after it was erected in 1959. The architect was Gerald Banks.

Hartland House, built in 1938 with a later extension to the right. Housing the library, one of the most extensive college libraries in Oxford, offices and common rooms, it is named after Mrs A.G. Hartland, to whom the college owes much for her important benefactions. Photograph taken in 1998.

Trenaman House, St Anne's newest building on site, taken in July 1997. The openings in the roof are for swifts. Built in 1994/95 it is named after Nancy Trenaman, a former Principal. By 1965 St Anne's owned all the houses on the south side of Bevington Road where once had lived Professors and dons.

Bicycles at St Anne's, July 1997. This is still the most convenient mode of travel around Oxford.

New and old at St Anne's college. Left to right: the circular south end of the Ogilvie Theatre, the Claire Palley building (student rooms), both named after former Principals, the Principal's house, 29 Banbury Road, and (over the wall) 27 Banbury Road. This pair of houses was designed by J.J. Stevenson, the latter for T.H. Green in 1882, Sadly, he died before they could move in but both his initials and those of his wife Charlotte are on the front of the house.

St Anne's is co-residential as this chalked rowing notice shows. The college arms are those of Field Marshal Plumer whose daughter Eleanor was once Principal. In the days when women's colleges were all single-sex there was a story of women being told about a man, and the Somerville woman asked 'What is he reading?', the St Hilda's one asked 'What is his school?', St Hugh's 'What does he play?', LMH 'Who are his people?'; but the St Anne's woman asked 'Where *is* he?'.

Three St Anne's graduates at a 'Words and Music' evening in January, 1998. Left to right: Elizabeth Jennings, poet, Penelope Lively, writer, and Janet Henfrey, actress. Elizabeth Jennings and Penelope Lively both grew up in North Oxford. In her poem *Anglo-Saxon* Elizabeth tells how she was asked to translate a piece of Beowulf in a week's time. 'Having no knowledge of Anglo-Saxon, I nearly went down my first day up.' Fortunately, she stayed.

## St Antony's

Initially funded by a benefaction of the Frenchman, M. Antonin Besse of Aden, the College came into existence in May 1950 and became a full graduate college of Oxford University in December 1963.

The college occupies buildings, designed by C. E. Buckeridge and J.L. Pearson (built 1866–94) for the Convent of the Society of the Holy and Undivided Trinity (SHUT). It was described by the architect W. Butterfield as 'the best modern building in Oxford after my college Keble.' Seen above, on the corner of Woodstock and Bevington Roads, in 1868, there were at that time no buildings between it and the church of St Philip and St James.

The college as it is today. (Photograph courtesy of St. Antony's College.) In 1946 the main old convent building housed Halifax House, a social centre for graduates, which moved to South Parks Road and is now incorporated into the University Club. During the Second World War the Royal Navy and a Free French detatchment had occupied it.

The Hilda Besse building, the first to be purpose-built for the college (1968/70), was named for the Founder's widow and opened by the Chancellor of the University, Harold Macmillan, in 1970. Thought to be on the site of an early Roman settlement and later a gravel pit and market garden, circuses were once held here. Nearby 1–5 Church Walk, 64–70, 83–85 and 86 and 107 Woodstock Road and 21, 22, 24 and 25/26 Winchester Road built in the 1870s and 1880s, are now all part of the college. Photograph taken in July 1997.

Mr Mike Dean, the Head Porter at St Antony's, taken in 1998. Note the old convent windows behind.

The library at St Antony's, refurbished in 1995, was once the convent chapel. It is a college of graduates and it is the only one in Oxford where overseas students outnumber those from the United Kingdom. In 1996, for instance, there were 98 students from 37 different countries. (Photograph courtesy of St Antony's College.)

How the Refectory looked at the time when the nuns lived in the convent and ran the schools there.

The Refectory as it is today, now called the Gulbenkian Reading Room (refurnished in 1991) at St Antony's.

The most recent building at St Antony's College. Built in 1992/3, the Nissan Institute from the east in Winchester Road. The original stone wall has been retained. Photograph taken in July 1997.

The Nissan building from the west. A new accommodation block is to be constructed to the right, on the site of squash and tennis courts.

## Green College

Green College was opened in 1979 and is a graduate college. It includes as part of its buildings the old Radcliffe Observatory, seen in this print of St Giles Field in 1781 from the site of St Anne's College.

The Observatory in 1834.

The Observatory from the east as it is today. It was built in 1772—95 by H. Keene and J. Wyatt. The upper octagon is a copy of the Tower of the Winds in Athens. The sculptures of the winds and the signs of the Zodiac are by J.C.F. Rossi, R.A. The premises were taken over by the Radcliffe Infirmary in 1935 when the Observatory moved to South Africa. In the grounds of the college there is equipment (now run by the School of Geography) which records the daily weather, the longest existing in England.

The entrance to Green College in Woodstock Road. This photograph was taken in July 1997, from the west. The college is named for Dr and Mrs Cecil Green of Dallas, Texas. Dr Green was born in Lancashire but his family emigrated to Canada when he was young. He founded his firm, Texas Instruments, and his benefaction enabled the college to be built and established. The first graduate entered in 1979. In 1980 a residential block designed by Jack Lankester was added.

Dr Cecil Green naming the College Ladies First VIII boat on 23rd June 1994. The college had recently rowed Head of the River in Eights. The boat was named in memory of Dr Green's late wife, Ida. A new men's boat was paid for partly by the Ida and Cecil Green Foundation and partly by the college and named the Cecil Green. On the right is Sir Crispin Tickell, Warden of Green College, 1990–1997. (Photograph courtesy of Alan Wiles and Green College).

Green College, 29th June 1998, on the occasion of the meeting of the College Advisory Council of which HRH The Princess Royal is a member. Seen here is the Warden, Sir John Hanson, KCMG, CBE, introducing the Princess Royal to (left to right): Phil Whittaker, Head Porter, Sandra Kimber (Housekeeper) and John Cooper, Chef. (Photograph courtesy of Bryant Gilot and Green College)

Many undergraduates from colleges in central Oxford are housed in North Oxford. This is Stevens Close in Woodstock Road, built for Lincoln College in 1973/4. The architect was John Fryman of the Architects Design Fellowship. Photograph taken in July 1997.

Trinity College annexe on the north corner of Staverton Road. It replaced a single house and now accommodates over 70 members of the college. Built in 1979, the architect was Simon Shew of Grey and Baynes. Photograph taken in January, 1988.

The house, 106 Woodstock Road, which once stood on the site of the Trinity College annexe and was the home of the Moylan family from 1939–1947. They rented it from Miss J. Payne. Rosalind and Dennis Moylan are in the left-hand photograph and Rosalind and Edwina Moylan in the right. For further information about this house and the Payne family who lived here from 1924/25, see Section 7.

94 Woodstock Road on the north corner of Rawlinson Road which was built in 1888 to the designs of H.G.W. Drinkwater. It is now named Ogston House after a former President of Trinity College which acquired the property. It was the subject of a key decision by Oxford City Council Planning Committee who refused to allow it to be demolished for development by Techomes. The Inspector at the subsequent inquiry refused permission and the decision was upheld. The house was, from 1954 to about 1968/9, the home of the Nobel prizewinner, Professor Dorothy Hodgkin OM, FRS (1910–1994), Hon. Fellow of Somerville (see page 37) and her husband Thomas. They had two sons and one daughter.

92 Woodstock Road on the southern corner of Rawlinson Road, taken in 1998. At one time part of the Squirrel School (see page 74), it is now the University of Oxford Department for Continuing Education. It was opened in 1992 and was then called W.K. Kellogg House but is now known as 92 Woodstock Road to avoid confusion with the main site of the Department for Continuing Education and Kellogg College situated at Rewley House.

## The Convent Schools

The fifth form room at St Michael's School which later, in 1965, became part of St Antony's College. The Society of the Holy and Undivided Trinity (S.H.U.T.) was founded in 1849 and the nuns of the Society moved into their new building on the corner of Woodstock Road and Bevington Road in March, 1868. They were previously at 24 St John Street. Designed by Buckeridge (see page 48), it cost £8,000 to build. St Michael's, which had been established in 1862, before the move to the Convent, went to Cirencester in 1930 and closed in 1951.

Mother Marian (formerly Marian Rebecca Hughes) who lived from 1817 to 1912 was sanctioned by Bishop Wilberforce of Oxford to found her sisterhood in 1849. She was the first person to become a sister of the Church of England. She educated children to a more advanced level than the Dame schools of that time. She gathered round her a group of women in order to build a community and to work for charity and education. She designed their habit of black with blue facings. In all, four schools were founded. In 1852, Mother Marian started her industrial school with the object of assisting girls aged 11 to 19 who, on leaving parish schools, could not find employment. Some day pupils, some boarders, the girls' studies prepared them for domestic service and home duties.

During the great cholera epedemic of October 1854, Mother Marian and her sisters nursed families in tents on Port Meadow under the guidance of Dr Acland.

A St Michael's school-room in the Convent (now part of St Antony's). In July 1857, Mother Marian began Holy Trinity Convent School, later known as St Denys, of which Dr Pusey was the first manager. By 1876, the school had moved into their new buildings in Winchester Road. Because they moved in on 9th October, St Denys' day, this is what the school was called. The buildings were later demolished for St Antony's.

Side by side in the Convent building were the Orphanage School where they learnt housework and St Michael's which was fee-paying and for the daughters of clergymen and other so-called 'gentry'. The orphans, distinguished by their pink dresses in summer and brown coats with red hoods in winter, were not allowed to speak to the St Michael's girls. The orphans liked to help the Sisters' handyman drive their herd of cows along the Woodstock Road for milking in the Convent grounds. The orphans, who had jobs such as serving, cleaning and doing laundry in the Convent, were later mostly children whose fathers were killed in the First World War.

Girls at the Convent of the Holy and Undivided Trinity taken in the garden with their teacher in about 1910. Far right, front row, is Annie Mary James whose daughter and grandaughter went to St Denys, the name the school took later.

Standard IV at the Holy and Undivided Trinity School in 1924. It was by then informally known as St Denys. Some orphan girls in their pink pinnies are also in the group. In 1945 the sisters handed over the school to the parish of St Philip and St James. It received aided status in 1953.

Standard V of the Holy and Undivided Trinity in 1924.

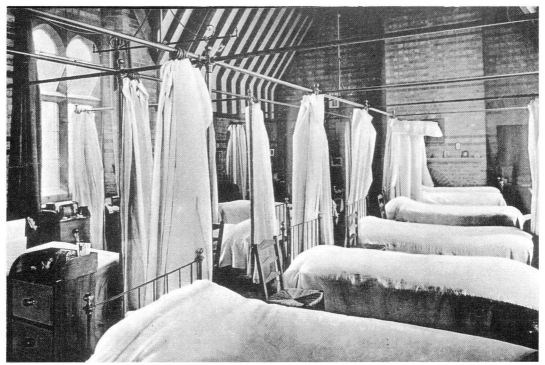

St Angelus dormitory in which the girls of St Michael's slept. They were aged 1 to 16 and many of them had parents who were abroad working in the Colonies. (All Convent school photographs courtesy of Molly Eagle, Kathleen White and Eileen Wright.)

Part of Class 1 at St Denys School in June 1963. The school closed that year. (Photograph courtesy of the Oxford *Mail and Times*.) Back row: unknown. Third row, left to right: –, Sharon Robb, –, Amanda Kingston. Second row: Ann West, Sally Lay, Violet Child, Venetia Taylor, –, –, –. Front row: Caroline Raby, Dedi Ashdown, –, Fiona Barker, Anita Blake. In December 1987, when Ann West and her husband and children were in the Philipines, she was confronted by a burglar in her house who stabbed and killed her.

## St Faith's

St Faith's was an offshoot of St Denys begun on 6th October 1900. Sister Margaret Isabel left St Denys School with some of the girls to found St Faith's. As 6th October is St Faith's Day that is what it was called. It started at 10 (and then 13) Bevington Road but finally became established, in December 1919, at 115 Woodstock Road.

St Faith's School Senior house, 115 Woodstock Road. The Junior School was next door at No. 117 which was bought for the school in 1943 but could not be used until the ATS (women's army) moved out. Then 60 juniors moved in. The school closed in 1965 and the houses were eventually demolished for Butler Close. Many of the girls told the vicar of the parish that they owed everything to St. Faith's. It was a happy school thoughout its existence and it was with great sadness that it closed when the leases of the houses were due to expire in 1966 and could not be renewed.

In the front row of this group, taken in 1928, are Sister Mary Hilary (left) and Sister Muriel. Some of the girls are in Girl Guides' uniform. At school they wore navy-blue tunics (later maroon) and maroon blazers with hat bands of maroon and grey. In summer they wore pink frocks. In the early days of the school at No. 115 the girls were told that they could only use the swing if they had their backs to the neighbours so that their legs and petticoats could not be seen over the wall. In earlier years the teachers were nuns and their devotion and quiet care and kindness were much appreciated.

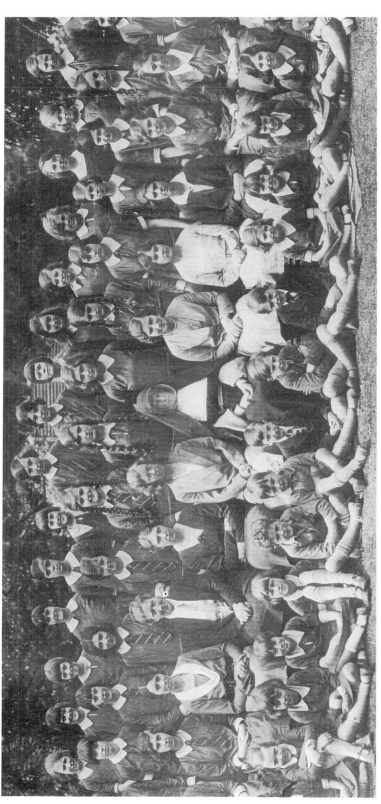

Part of a large group at St Faith's School in 1932. The dresses were maroon. Until 1943, small boys were also taken. It was not until 1942 that there was a lay headmistress. Miss Joyce Pollard (who is in the photograph) remembers on the occasion of a Nativity play, when she was off-stage drinking cocoa, a mistress rushed urgently towards her asking: 'Where are those blasted angels?' Back row, left to right: –, –, Cicely Dyer, –, –, – Le Conte, Peggy Bowles, Barbara Twining, –, Kathleen Puttick, –, Margaret Pelda, –, June Davis, –. Third row: Peggy Filer, Jeanne Hawkins, –, Joan Beasley, Betty Skelcher, –, – Kate Hodinett, Muriel Loose, Joyce Pollard, –, –, –. Second row: Ghreta Park, Miss Park Smith (French teacher), Miss Reeve, Miss Drake (who taught juniors), Miss West (art, literature, drama and sports), Sister Muriel (headmistress and taught history), Miss Nellie Organ (games and juniors), Miss Bent, Miss Horwood (maths and botany), Head Girl, –. Front row: the only one identified is Marjorie Bristow, eighth from left. (Photograph courtesy of Miss Joyce Pollard.)

## St Paul's School

Built in 1847/48 St Paul's School, the site of which was given by the Radcliffe Trustees, was at 119a Walton Street. (Photograph taken in 1998). It was restored by H.W. Moore in 1888 and is a Grade II listed building. There had been a school for 70 girls and some infants from at least 1837 but they were taught in a small hired room. Within seven years of this school being built there were 250 children, taught by a certificated mistress and an assistant mistress and six pupil teachers. In 1854 a boys' school was started in Great Clarendon Street. The girls remained at St Paul's until 1876 when it closed.

There was also Bedford House School in Walton Streeet, near to Little Clarendon Street. It held reunions long after it closed.

## St Philip and St James School

A group of infants with their teachers at St Philip and St James School in Leckford Road taken at the turn of the century. (Photograph courtesy of Mr Colin Harris). For some years after the formation of the parish in 1863 children attended St Giles' School but by early 1873 the Leckford Road building was ready for the infants to move in. It was enlarged in 1888 to take 159 children. When boys were no longer taken at the Holy Trinity Convent school a new building was erected for them next to the infants' school here in 1879. It was rebuilt in 1896 and additions made in 1933.

In its early years when the whole school met together in the big hall the children sat in what were known as galleries which were raked platforms of floors with bars in the front on which they placed their slates or books.

School fees were paid regularly and collected by the Treasurer or his representative. It was very much a Church school with holidays given on major festivals and Saints' days but the main holidays were short; for instance, only a month in mid-summer, a week in late September and early October and a fortnight at Christmas. When St Giles' Fair was on, the children were given the afternoon off.

Inspectors came regularly and sent written comments. That of October 1874 included: 'The school is taught with great kindness and in many respects with skill; handwriting too small and cramped. Arithmetic rather weak.' In 1882 in answer to a query as to whether boys as well as girls did needlework (if a grant were to be claimed for both) it was agreed that both should do sewing and knitting. At the 1889 prizegiving three boys won a prize for a 'knife cloth' and two for a knitted, woollen scarf. These were presented to them at the Town Hall by the Countess of Jersey.

A Mayday group at St Philip and St James. Date not known. (Photograph courtesy of Mr Colin Harris).

A class of infants in 1921. Third row, second from left is James Walter Holt who died suddenly from meningitis when he was 16½. Second row, second left is Enid Messenger. The teacher is Miss Sampson.

Children at St Philip and St James School in about 1932. It was a tradition for children to take along some of their own favourite toys for the group photograph (courtesy Mr John Smith who is seated on a chair in the back row, third from left.).

There was strict discipline as well as kindness and a verse circulated in the school in the 1930s about the then head of school, Mr George C. Dent.

*Mr Dent is a very good man,*
*He goes to church on Sundays*
*Where he prays to God*
*To give him strength*
*To cane the boys on Mondays.*

Despite this description of Mr Dent, whom the children called 'Gaffer', when he retired the children contributed to buy him a bicycle.

A class at St Philip and St James under the chestnut tree in 1933. Note the toys again. Second row: far left Jean Ward, third from left Audrey Mary Harris (née Smith), eighth from left Margaret Collier. (Photograph courtesy of Mr Colin Harris).

A class at St Philip and St James in about 1927. Back row, left to right: Daisy Barson, —, Flossie Fathers, Stuart —, Miss Brucker (teacher). Fourth row: —, Dorothy Clark, Joyce Paddock, Shiela Thomas, Betty Bird. Third row: —, Margaret Giles, —, Gracie Smith, Eileen —, —, Joan Watts, Eileen Wall, Iris Rawlins, Charlie Molynieux. Second row: Aubrey Maaz, —, —, Harry Nut, Stuart —, Eric Bustin. Front row: —, —, —, — Wall, Olive Smith, Ralph Tuffrey, —.

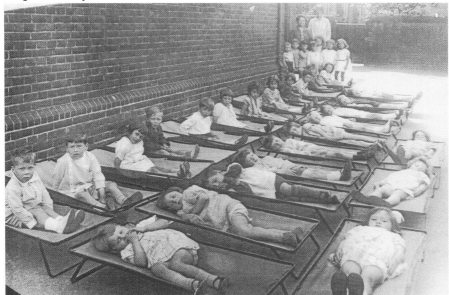

A group of infants resting in the afternoon at St Philip and St James School. Standing at the back are (left) Miss Ward and Miss Brucker, teachers, with (left to right) four unidentified children, Daisy Barson, Aubrey Maaz and Eileen —. Back row, left to right: —, Stuart —, Betty Bird, Charles Molynieux, Harry Nut, Shiela Thomas, Flossie Fathers, Gracie Smith, Eric Bustin, —, Iris Rawlings. Right-hand row, top to bottom: Eileen Wall, —, Joan Watts (now Mrs Heaven, who kindly lent the above two photographs).

By 1965 Bishop Kirk School and The Cherwell School, further north, had taken the older pupils and the Leckford Road premises were modernised and adapted to re-open in 1966 as an infant school.

A mural in the playground, February 1988

St Philip and St James School is looked upon as a focal point for the residents of Walton Manor, particularly for those with children there, and it is very much part of the community.

## St Aloysius School

This school started in 1881 next to the church of the same name at the southern end of the Woodstock Road. In 1892 it was rebuilt so that it could take as many as 80 boys. In 1932 it began to take girls as well and became a junior mixed school. The photograph shows the school building in its last year on the church site in 1957. In that year the roof of the building was raised and a hall built over it. The two school rooms are now parish offices. (This photograph and that opposite courtesy of Mr and Mrs P. Selwood). The school moved to its new site further north on the corner of St Margaret's and Woodstock Roads in 1971/2.

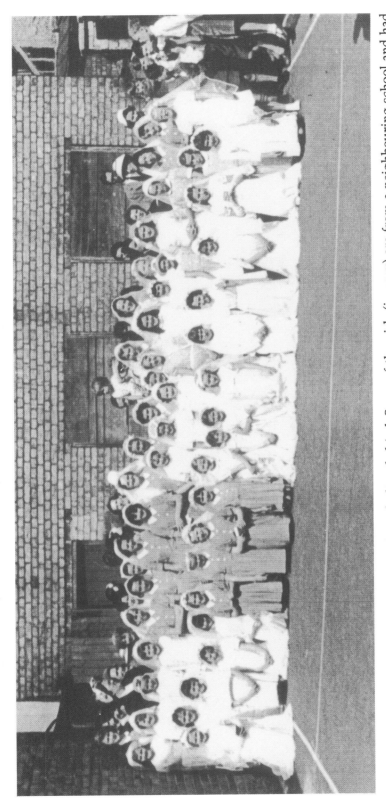

The girls of St Aloysius School, with the boys hiding behind. Some of the girls (in grey) are from a neighbouring school and had joined in the procession which took place that day. The building behind has since been replaced by one for Somerville College.

The front entrance of St Aloysius School, July 1998.

The Headmaster of St Aloysius School, Mr Chris Crouch, with Oak class teacher Mrs Maxine Baker and (left to right) Teisa Urriolagoitia, Joseph Richings and Jason Lee. Taken in Oak classroom in July, 1998.

A group of children at St Aloysius School, July 1998. Back row: Sophie Connolly, Hannah Kagum, Rosie Magnay, Katie Dennehy, Coln Flaherty. Front row: Madeleine Bowden, Tessa Campbell, Cherelle Gayle, Joshua Bowden.

The Headmaster of St Aloysius School, Mr Chris Crouch, with, back row: Oliver Richardson, Marain Lubowieki, Marion Rawlings. Front row: Teisa Urriolagoitia, Joseph Richings, Tessa Campbell, Emma Gibbons, Prima Sakuntabhi, Elke Horner.

## The Squirrel School

The Squirrel School, 90 Woodstock Road, taken in 1998.

It is probably true to say that there have been and still are more schools in a square mile of North Oxford than any other place. Some only lasted for a few decades, others have already reached their century. One which has been thriving for over 50 years is the Squirrel School.

Miss Sally Bell, the founder and first head of the Squirrel School, taken in May 1998. Miss Bell started the school in some converted stables behind 13a Rawlinson Road in September 1947 with just three children aged between 2 and 4 years old. The daughter of a Fellow of Balliol, she had never intended to start a school but just a playgroup when she was between jobs.

By 1949 larger premises were required and the school moved to 92 Woodstock Road where about 30 children attended from 9 a.m. to 4 p.m. with a cooked midday dinner. Children were able to stay until they were seven years old and some boarders were taken in the 1950s. Miss Bell's lawyer, who had had little faith in her, a young girl in her 20s with a severe stammer, with no capital and a huge mortgage on a leasehold house, had given her venture 'five years at the most and then you will be ruined.' However, he had soon been proved wrong.

The name came about in an interesting way. Within a few years of starting what was at first called 'Miss Bell's', by coincidence another Miss Bell started a group in North Oxford. Sally Bell writes: "I called my little ones together and told them that we must find a new name for ourselves. 'But we have a name already,' they said. 'We are called the Squirrel School because of the squirrel that lives in the tree in our playground and calls to visit us each day."

Children at the Squirrel School in the early 1950s. Left to right: Andrew Harvey (climbing up), Celia Toynbee, Richard Helsby, Jaun Vizoso, Anita Clarke, Linda Harrison.

A class being read to by Ms O'Leary in the 1950s. Back row, left to right: Arf Khen, Simon Johnson, Nicholas Jones. Front row: Matthew Wheatley, –, Eleanor Williamson, Ben Woodward, Elizabeth Phillips.

A performance of Robin Hood by children of the Squirrel School in about 1971. Richard Tyler (left) as Robin, is speaking to the Sheriff.

Edward Phelps as Robin Hood's man (right) meeting a village girl.

In 1970 Miss Bell was diagnosed as having severe nerve deafness which could not be cured but she overcame this disability enough to continue as Head until 1984. Having sold No. 92 to the Oxford and County Secretarial School in 1979, the Squirrel had been able to buy the freehold of No. 90. In 1984 the school was sold to Mr and Mrs D. Eaton and on their retirement in 1996 it was amalgamated with the Oxford High School for Girls. At the present time (1998), there are 126 boys and girls. In 1999 it is intended that they should be taken from three to seven years old, it being the pre-prep school with Greycotes for Juniors and the High School for Seniors.

## Rothesay House School

This school, at 189 Woodstock Road, started its life in 1918 and in that year was called Rothesay Anglo-French School. By the following year it had dropped the words 'Anglo-French' from the title. It was run by Mrs Hickling, Principal, and her daughter Miss Hickling. It became a day and boarding school for girls and a kindergarten for boys and girls from 5 years. Peggy Rees (née Stobo), who was a weekly boarder at the school in 1921, remembers Mrs Hickling as a 'nice lady, rather stout, who wore long black dresses and long necklaces.' In due course she was assisted by her three daughters, Dolly. Ethel and Jessie. Nellie Reynolds was Matron. The girls wore navy-blue gym slips and white blouses with berries in winter and light-blue check gingham dresses and panama hats in summer. Reunions were held until fairly recently. Special subjects taught were needlework and ballroom dancing. The girls put on dancing shows at the old Playhouse in Woodstock Road. By 1949 Mrs Salkeld took over as Principal. The school closed in about 1954. The house, which was built in 1904 to the designs of H.W. Moore, is now converted into flats.

Girls of the VIth form at Rothesay House at the end of their school term in 1938 with their cups and shield. Back row: Pat Goodbrand, Veronica —, Mellasina —, Jean Pasmore In front (with shield): Barbara Pickford. (Photograph courtesy of Mrs Jean Saunder (née Pasmore).

**Notre Dame**

Numbers 145 and 147 Woodstock Road, two of three houses which made up Notre Dame School. They were built in 1888/9 and the architects were Wilkinson and Moore. Between the houses is the chapel which was built in the late 1930s.

The school was planned in the late 1930s but then the Second World War came. Number 143 was occupied by nurses from the Radcliffe Infirmary but the school was able to begin at No. 147 with 11 children. The High School, with children starting at 11 years old, was not begun until 1949 and a sixth form was added (for girls up to 18 years) in 1950. Number 147 then became a prep school for boys and girls (5 to 11 years) which, when it outgrew that building moved across the road to No. 84 where Hartley Court is now (built 1971/2). Rye St Anthony School, now at Headington, was once here. Both schools were run and taught by the Catholic sisters of the Community of Notre Dame which is a world-wide organisation. In 1972 the High School moved to Cowley, where it was amalgamated with Salesians School, and to the middle school in Marston Ferry Road. Number 143 was pulled down for St Aloysius Roman Catholic First School.

The Sisters of Notre Dame still live at 145 and 147 Woodstock Road. Here some of them are seen taking tea at the Convent with Mother Teresa of Calcutta in 1988. Left to right: Sr Margaret Taylor, Sr Margaret Goodier, Mother Teresa, Sr Catherine Chapman and a companion of Mother Teresa. (Convent photographs courtesy of the Sisters of Notre Dame.)

## Woodstock House School

Woodstock House School, 108 Woodstock Road, began in the 1920s and ended in the early 1950s. For the whole of that time, the founder, Miss Florence Tucker was Head, ably assisted over many years by Miss Hawkins, Miss Baines and Miss Tyrrell. Her sister was Housekeeper. Miss Trafford, who played the piano for P.E. classes, lived to be nearly a 100. It was a day school for girls and boys up to the age of 11 years, mostly from North Oxford. The school provided a good basic education for children who went on to Oxford schools such as the Girls' and Boys' High Schools. It had a pleasant and popular garden where, in fine weather, lessons were held under the apple trees. The house still survives, next to the Trinity College annexe.

A group of children at Woodstock House School in 1940/41. In the back row are David Welford (left) and Hugh Wyllie. Standing in front is Richard Parker.

Woodstock House School, a group taken in about 1942. Back row, left to right: Robin Hall, John Cave, Stella Welford, Peter Bull. Front row: Malcolm Brooks, Betty Green, Daphne Parker (now Mrs Fitchett), Ann Gass. (Both photographs courtesy of Miss Stella Welford).

# *The Community*

## St Margaret's Institute

St Margaret's Institute (photograph taken in 1997) was the first house to be built in Polstead Road. It was started as a Working Men's Institute by some wealthy parishioners of St Philip and St James Church in 1889, the land being leased from St John's College. The club for working men was open from 2 p.m. each day and there was provision for cards, darts, chess and dominoes. The billiards room was exceptionally large and so fine that the Oxford Billiards League held their championship matches there. The club, the members of which had to apply and be sponsored, was about 150 strong. It especially thrived in the 1930s. The men would have worked at Lucy's Ironworks, the University Press or on the railway. The Club ceased to exist after the 1939/45 War when people found other pursuits but the premises are still used and valued by those who live locally and beyond.

## Walton Manor Residents' Association

The Association is a thriving organisation which has been in existence since 1972. The photograph shows present and immediate past members of the Committee taking refreshment after their 1998 Annual General Meeting which was held at St Philip and St James School. Back row, left to right: Simon Price, Bill Tollett (Hon. Treasurer), David van Oss. Second row: Peter Strong, Micky Moerian, Mary Bull, Diana Senior, Councillor Jean Fooks. Front row: Sarah Wood, Graham Broughton (Chair), Tilly Flynn (Hon. Secretary). The Residents' Association is open to anyone living in the area between the Radcliffe Infirmary and the south side of Farndon Road, including the west side of Woodstock Road and across to the canal. The east side of Walton Street to St Bernard's Road, Kingston and Southmoor Roads are also included.

## The St Margaret's Area Society

The Society holds regular meetings and includes not only that road but Farndon Road and the northern end of Kingston Road. Its Chair is Councillor Dermot Roaf and the Hon. Secretary is Dr Tim King.

## The Big Game Museum

The former Big Game Museum in Woodstock Road, known as the Red Barn, which housed the Playhouse Theatre from 23rd October 1923. The theatre closed in 1938, the year in which it moved to Beaumont Street. *The Daily Telegraph* Drama critic wrote: 'If a repertory theatre cannot succeed in a great University town it can surely hope to succeed nowhere.' The Red Barn had its ups and downs, despite good casts, because there were many competing attractions in term-time. The undergraduate magazine Isis wrote of one performer there: 'He may become a fine actor – he has it in him – if he works and does not fall victim to easy success.' The actor was John Gielgud. Next door in the photograph, taken in 1997, can be seen the St Giles Parish Room built in 1887/91 the architect of which was H.W. Moore.

The Red Barn was converted to a Workshop for people with disabilities by Oxford City Council. In the front was what was known as 'The Blind and Handicapped Shop'. Many North Oxford people relied on the excellent re-caning of chairs, mending of watches and so on which were undertaken by people with visual and physical handicaps until it closed in 1984. The building was then taken over by OISE, the Oxford Intensive School of English, and an extension to the north replaced an old house. Then in 1992 the Language Centre of Oxford University came there. Started in 1980, it had formerly been at 41 Wellington Square. Under the Directorship of Dr Robert Vandeplank, the Centre today has between 1,500 and 3,000 users per annum with 200 hours of classes a week. A total of 103 different languages are taught.

Ironwork in the roof space of the old Big Game Museum and former theatre. (Courtesy of the Language Centre, University of Oxford.)

Taube Marks, Librarian of the Language Centre seated in a language booth by the theatre's old proscenium arch.

## Wyndham House

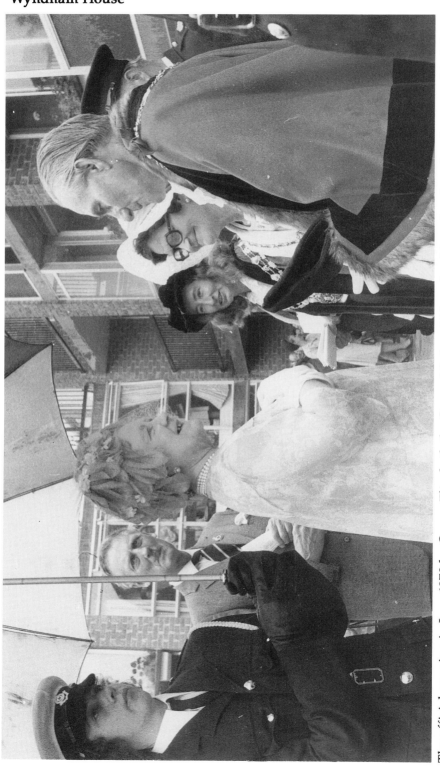

The official opening in June 1973 by Queen Elizabeth the Queen Mother. Although taking place in a thunderstorm this did not dampen the joy of the occasion. The Queen Mother is talking to the Lord Mayor, Alderman Fred Ingram, who had helped to finance the scheme which was a project of the British Red Cross to celebrate its centenary. It replaced a Home for elderly people in Banbury Road and consists of self-contained flats for rent with meals provided and a warden in charge. The site was provided by St John's College. It was named for a former President of the Branch. On the right in the photograph is the Lady Mayoress and on her right is the Sheriff of Oxford, Alderman Ann Spokes.

Deserted seats in the storm at Wyndham House on opening day whilst speeches are made from a make-shift shelter. The heavy rain penetrated the awning and dripped onto the hat of the Lady in Waiting, Lady Jean Rankin, seated behind the speaker. The Lord Mayor and Sheriff can be seen sheltering from the rain round the corner where also were standing the Duke and Duchess of Marlborough.

Wyndham House, Leckford Road frontage in April 1998. All formal connection with the Red Cross ended in 1976. The house has its own management committee.

## North Oxford Cricket Club

The North Oxford Cricket Club played on St John's College playing fields in Woodstock Road from 1902 to 1995. It was founded in 1900 and became one of the strongest City clubs, winning the Airey Cup in 1923. In the late 1940s an Australian member of the Club took all 11 wickets in a 12-a-side match at Tiddington. The famous cricketer, Jack Hobbs, played against the club and was given out lbw for 17.

This photograph was taken on the day of the President's match in 1931. Back row, left to right: Jack Thompson, Dudley Goodey, W. Allen, T. Allen, Monty Money, H.G. Webb, Harry Champion, Colin Franks. Middle row: N. Seddon, A. Chamberlain, T. Fisher, T. Towell (Scorer), C. Wyatt, Jack Godfrey, Percy Thompson, Eric Bowtell, B. Ferriman, L. Rogers, David Money [in front of T. Towell] (Scorer). Front row: E. Tucker, J. Evans, F. Draper, Herbert Halliday, W. Walters (President), B. Rogers, two scorers (names not known).

On about the only two good summer days in 1954 they were visited by a South African side. They were the first club in Oxford to start Cricket weeks. Photographs are courtesy of Richard Pineo who has written a good history of the club (1900–1995).

On the occasion of the President's XI game on 3rd September 1995, the last match to be played on St John's College ground. Back row, left to right: Darryl Woods (Vice-Captain 1995), Chris Clements (former Captain), Roger Busby (former Captain), David Wise (Captain 1995). Front row: Alan Crossley (former Captain), Roy Surman (former Captain), Bob Boyles (Chairman 1995), Richard Pineo (President 1995).

There was an excellent bowls green on the ground nearest to Bainton Road. Three cricketers also played bowls and Eric Bowtell (who ran the Scala Cinema in Walton Street), Bert Halliday and Basil Rogers won the English Triples Championship in 1951. The North Oxford Tennis Club was also at the ground for many years until it moved to Banbury Road North. The grass courts were some of the best in Oxford.

SECTION FOUR

# Churches

St Philip and St James Church, Woodstock Road, built in 1860–62. The steeple was added in 1864–66 and this photograph was taken soon afterwards. The architect was G.E. Street. The vicarage to the south at 68 Woodstock Road was not built until 1887 (see Section 1). (Photograph courtesy of Oxford Architectural and Historical Society).

A group outside the Church in the First World War. Mrs Strode Jackson and (possibly) her son together with admiring youngsters. Third from left in the background is Annie Pimm, later Mrs Harris. (This and the photograph below courtesy of Mr Colin Harris).

Baptism card of 1939 presented to Philip Arthur Smith by the Vicar.

St Philip and St James (affectionately known as Phil and Jim) in its present-day leafy setting (Photograph taken in 1997.) Note that the clock was not in the earlier picture but now, with its many faces, it is very much part of the North Oxford scene.

John Ogg seen here with his daughter and her bridesmaids on the day of her wedding in 1966 arriving at St Philip and St James Church. Mr Ogg (still going strong at 91), who did everything for love, climbed the tower every day for many years in order to undertake the heavy job of winding the clock by hand. The Vicar of the day, the Reverend Max Saint, thought Mr Ogg should be saved this work and the clock was electrically wired by the firm which looked after Big Ben. Mr Ogg stoked the furnace too and when he was away his daughter Carol used to look after both the clock and the furnace. (Photographs courtesy of Mrs Carol Davis).

The parish became depopulated in the mid-1960s with many of the large houses standing empty as their leases were ending and colleges were waiting to buy them up. There were few 'real' households and the church lost its parochial status in 1972. It is now the Oxford Centre for Mission Studies which is the study and service centre for the Fellowship of Evangelical Mission Theologians. It prepares candidates for the Oxford University post-graduate certificate of theology. The building still retains most of its original interior.

St Margaret's Church on the corner of St Margaret's Road and Kingston Road was built in 1883—4 to the designs of H.G. Drinkwater. A local man, he had also designed St Philip and St James school and vicarage. With many new houses being built and the population growing, the existing church of St Philip and St James (built 20 years earlier) was insufficient for their needs. Drinkwater was asked to build a church to seat 500 people. Photograph taken in early Spring 1998.

There had been a shed in the Heyfield's Hutt area (see Section 6) which had been converted into a mission room and used since about 1875. Mother and daughter churches both flourished but in 1896 St Margaret's became independent of St Philip and St James to become a parish of its own. It was a very lively and active church with its own parish library, a parish wheelchair and a Horticultural Society.

There were originally plans for a tower by G.F. Bodley but it was not finished. This drawing, thought to come from Bodley's workshop, shows the tower as it might have been.

The Lady Chapel at St Margaret's. Drawing and photograph courtesy of the Churchwardens, St Margaret's.

Arising from the changes to the area (see St Philip and St James Church) the Oxford Deanery Synod produced a report in 1973 which suggested that the two parishes should be joined together again. Therefore in 1976 the two churches became a single unit officially entitled the Parish of St Philip and St James with St Margaret. It is now a thriving parish in the High Church tradition. Its strength comes from the fact that it has always been a neighbourhood church. In 1984 the benefice was united with that of St Giles.

The wedding of Dr David Smith, Churchwarden of St Margaret's, and Michèle Crawford on the 20th July 1985. He has been Librarian of St Anne's College since 1987 and she is Deputy Head of Wychwood School where she has taught since 1971. Photograph courtesy of Ms Michèle Crawford and Dr David Smith.

St Paul's Church, Walton Street, called by Pevsner 'the finest Grecian Church of Oxford', was built in 1835—6 in the Greek Classic style to the designs of H.J. Underwood.

The parish was reduced in size when St Barnabas parish, Jericho, was created in 1869. In 1866, for instance, the congregation of 600 could not increase because there was no room for them. It had become a popular centre for Tractarianism. Congregations were much reduced by the 1950s and the benefice was united with St Barnabas in 1963. The church closed in 1969, was abandoned and derelict in the 1970s and was then threatened with demolition. Fortunately, this was averted in 1979 when the church was acquired by the Oxford Area Arts Council (OAAC) and converted into a concert hall and theatre with the blessing of the Diocesan Redundant Churches Uses Committee. Money was raised by the St Paul's Appeal Support Fund and by 1981 the church had been restored and preserved. Many well-reviewed and well-patronised performances took place over the years until 1987 when OAAC Ltd, without the City Council support it had been receiving earlier, went into liquidation. The St Paul's Rescue Committee had hoped to buy the building so that performances could continue but they were outbid by Freud Lemos who opened the building in 1988 as a bar and cafe with performances of live music and occasional art exhibitions. Photograph taken in 1997.

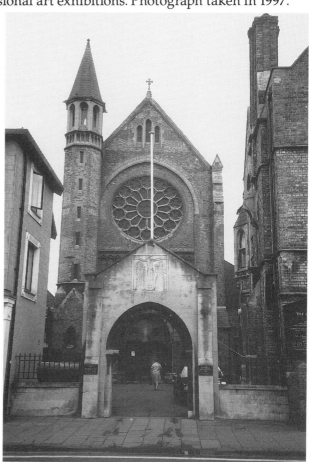

The Oratory, St Aloysius Church, Woodstock Road.

Built in 1873–5, the architect was Joseph A. Hansom (designer of the Hansom cab). It was opened in 1875 by Cardinal Manning. English Roman Catholics were not permitted by their church to attend the University until 1895 so that at first the majority of the congregation came from the town. The entrance to the church, shown here (1997) is from the east which is unusual but necessitated by the position of the site.

A painting by George Warner Allen (1972) in a side chapel at the Oratory. It represents the difficulties and disappointments associated with the building of the Oxford Oratory. The baby Jesus is seen pelting Cardinal John Henry Newman (seen kneeling) with stones. St Philip Neri is, however, intervening to prevent further stones being thrown. Newman, Vicar of St Mary's (1828—43) and a Fellow of Oriel was, with others, the founder of the Oxford Movement of the 1820s and early 1830s. He became a Roman Catholic, left Oxford in 1846 and set up the Birmingham Oratory in 1848. Oxford was one of the places in which he had hoped to set up an Oratory but it was not until 1993, three years after the centenary of his death, that the Oxford Oratory was established in this church. The Jesuits, whose church it had been, had already handed it over to the Birmigham Diocese in 1981.

The wedding of Mary Leahy and Patrick Selwood on 14th July 1951. Father Colvin is the priest. The High Altar, made of veined black marble, was moved forward in 1966. The church is full of statues and memorials of interest including a Holy-water stoup in memory of Gerard Manley Hopkins who, during his greatest poetic period, was a curate at St Aloysius.

A Requiem Mass held after the death of President J.F. Kennedy in 1963. In the foreground are three members of the American armed forces.

A group outside St Aloysius Church just before setting out on a pilgrimage to Lourdes in the 1960s. Father Lake is in the centre (in priest's clothing) and on his right (in beret) is Tim Selwood, Leader of the group. (The above three photogrphs courtesy of Mr and Mrs P. Selwood).

St Luke's Chapel, Radcliffe Infirmary. The original hospital chapel was a room above the Board Room but by 1862 it was thought a more worthy building should be erected. Thomas Combe, the local philanthropist, and superintendent of the Clarendon Press, offered to provide the chapel and appointed as architect Mr A.W. Blomfield (later Sir Arthur) who was the son of the Bishop of London. The cost was about £3,000. The consecration service, at which Bishop Wilberforce preached, was in June 1865. Combe was a Governor of the Infirmary and a member of the Board of Management from 1852 until his death in 1872.

The doorway of St Luke's showing a relief of Jesus the Good Shepherd. It is believed to be the work of Mr Earp.

# *The Radcliffe Infirmary*

The Radcliffe Infirmary in 1834, the date of this old print. It was as a result of the will of John Radcliffe that plans to build the Infirmary were first proposed. Thomas Rowney, M.P. for Oxford (1722–59) gave Coggins Piece, a five-acre site in the open fields of St Giles, on which to build it.

Radcliffe (1652–1714) was a member of University College, gaining his BM in 1675 and DM in 1682. He was physician to Mary II, William III and Queen Anne. Once when Queen Anne thought she was ill he told her that her trouble was 'imaginitis'.

From the begininning the Infirmary, which was opened on St Luke's day, 1770, was not just for City people and members of the University but took patients from Berkshire and Buckinghamshire as well as Oxfordshire. The building was designed by Stiff Leadbetter and originally had steps either side of the main entrance up which only Governors were allowed to enter.

The original seven rules of the hospital included: 'Every person subscribing one guinea may recommend one in-patient a year. Ladies who subscribe over three guineas can vote on all occasions.' By 1875, as a result of improvements made by Sir Henry Acland, 1,300 in-patients, 3,400 out-patients and 1,800 casualties were treated. By the time of the First World War the Infirmary was much increased in size.

Nurses with the Assistant Matron (centre, seated), Margaret Helen Anderson, at the turn of the century. She left in 1919 after 25 years service in that post. (Photograph courtesy of Dr E. Boardman and Oxfordshire Health Archives).

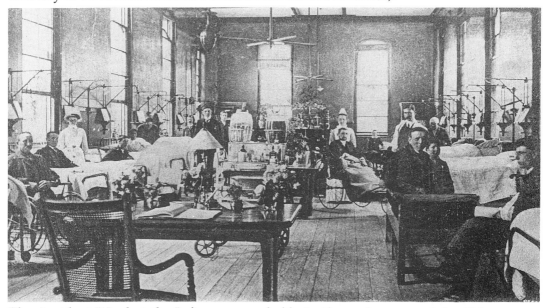

The Accident Ward at the Infirmary, probably in the early years of the 19th century. (Copyright Jeremy's, Oxford Stamp Centre).

The Radcliffe Infirmary before the new entrance was built in 1933. (For the chapel on the right see Section 4). The railings were erected in 1857.

The Triton fountain in the forecourt.

On 8th July 1857 a fountain committtee was appointed and made such good progress that a design was put before a Board meeting on 5th August and by the time the Annual Report for that year was presented the fountain was in place. The Treasurer of the Committee, the Reverend Thomas Briscoe, Vice-Principal of Jesus College, gave much of his own money towards the cost. Triton (the son of Poseidon (or Neptune) was a merman with a fish tail and a human body. There is no record of why the design was chosen. The sculptor, whose works grace many parts of London, was John Bell (b.1812). It was bought off the peg from a catalogue of J.M. Blashfield of Paddington which included 500 items including vases, busts and chimney pots. Made of baked clay (terracotta) it is modelled after the marble Triton in Rome's Piazza Barberini which was the work of Gian Lorenzo Bernini (1598–1680). Blashfield had supplied four great Tritons, among other pieces, to the Crystal Palace in 1854. The local water company agreed not to charge the Radcliffe Infirmary for the extra water used since it was said that it could be used for flushing drains or in the event of a fire.

In a hut near this fountain was the office of the first almoner of the Infirmary (from about 1920 to 1937), Miss Janet Payne.

HRH the Duchess of York visits Oxford's new Maternity Home at the Radcliffe Infirmary, the gift of Sir William Morris (later Lord Nuffield). The picture shows the two of them inspecting the new buildings on 22nd October 1931. The Matron (second from the right) was Miss Muriel Sparks. (Photograph courtesy of Dr E. Boardman and Oxfordshire Health Archives).

At the end of the 1930s, as a result of a large benefaction from Lord Nuffield, the hospital expanded into the Observatory grounds and medical education became properly established. In 1948 when the National Health Service came in, the management was under the United Oxford Hospitals Board of Governors. In 1972 the maternity services moved to the site in Headington which was to have the name of the John Radcliffe Hospital. The Infirmary remains a specialist teaching hospital but there are plans to relocate it to the John Radcliffe and Churchill hospital campuses by the year 2000.

Some of the benefactors whose names are on the walls of the Board Room. Not only are the donors' names given, written in gold lettering on a black background, but the amounts are also recorded.

Mrs Valerie Thompson, Personal Assistant to the Chairman of the Board and Chief Executive of the Radcliffe Infirmary, dressed for a special historical exhibition in the Board Room, September 1997.

A memorial plaque, above a former drinking fountain, which was re-erected in the front corridor of the Radcliffe Infirmary on 10th May 1998. Mrs Moyra Haynes, Secretary of the Oxford Preservation Trust, is seen here. The Trust contributed to the restoration of the plaque. The insciption says: 'In grateful memory of Ebenezer Wenham Alden MRCS who died August 22nd 1913 aged 63. The cost of this fountain was defrayed by a number of his patients and friends who desired to perpetuate the memory of a life singularly rich in the service of suffering humanity, Feb. 1914.' Descendants of the good and well-loved doctor were at the Infirmary to celebrate the restoration.

The Eye Hospital, which is on the same site as the Infirmary, was founded by Robert Walter Doyne in 1886. It was originally in Wellington Square but moved to its present site in 1894. The architect was Sir Arthur Blomfield who also designed St. Luke's chapel on the Woodstock Road frontage of the Infirmary (see Section 4). Ida Mann was mainly responsible for the re-building of the Eye Hospital and the nearby Nuffield Laboratory of Opthalmology. Made Reader in 1942, she went on to be the first woman Professor at Oxford University. She was created a Dame in 1980 for the excellent work which she did.

# *Public Houses*

The Royal Oak, 42/44 Woodstock Road, is opposite the Radcliffe Infirmary and therefore for many years has been patronised by doctors and nurses. When the Playhouse was a few houses down the road the pub was also popular with actors. Despite 17th and 18th century alterations, it is the oldest pub in the area. The name is derived from an ancient oak tree in a nearby medieval field called 'shooting glebe'. John Morris and his son Thomas, who lived in one of the cottages on the original site, repaired the wheels of passing coaches, carts and waggons. While this was being done Mrs Morris and her daughters served refreshments to passing travellers and this developed into a hostelry and the public house of today.

The Plume of Feathers in Observatory Street was named after the insignia of the Prince of Wales. It was established in 1881 and had its own villa and garden. There had been a pub of the same name at 38 George Street. Neither pub or villa now exist because they were demolished in 1935 and replaced by Belsyre Court.

Mr Searle ('The Boss'), seen seated with his wife Emma (née Jones), ran the Plume and Feathers in the 1920s. Their daughters are, left to right: Doris (Waine), Monica (Skinner) and Mliss (Bradfield). The photograph was taken in 1925 in front of the Searle's cottage.

The Wedding of Doris Searle and Sidney Waine in about 1922. Photographs courtesy of Mrs Joan Bates.

The Horse and Jockey, 69 Woodstock Road on the northern corner of St Bernard's Road.

An earlier inn was established here in 1750 and it became the headquarters of the stewards of the horse races held on Port Meadow. It is said that from about 1804 the horses were shown here before continuing on to the races. Prior to about 1829 the road (now St Bernard's but before that St John's Road) was called Horse and Jockey Lane. It was down a track on the line of this road in June 1644 that Charles I escaped from Oxford, together with 6,000 of his troops. The wheels of the carts and the horses' hooves were muffled and it is said that no one told the Cromwellian forces. When, in 1879, Morrells' Brewery took over the lease from the owners, St John's College, they rebuilt the pub to the designs of H.G. Drinkwater. In the early 20th century there were stables at the back of the pub which housed the beautiful white horses belonging to Mrs White.

The landlady of the Horse and Jockey in 1918 when her husband, Bernard Busby Snr, was in the Services. She is seen with her children (left to right) Ron, Doris (who later married Frank Collar, oar maker), Bernard Jnr, Mrs Ann Busby, Mary. (Photograph courtesy of Mrs Paula Simms.) The Busbys were still running the pub in 1935. It was refurnished in the open-plan style in about 1988 and is popular with the many students in the area.

The Moulders' Arms was at 39 St Bernard's Road. It opened in 1872 but ceased to be an inn by 1939 when it became a private house. It was much patronised by men who worked at the nearby Lucy's Ironworks who would quench their thirst there after pouring the molten metal into moulds for casting, hence the name. This photograph was taken in 1997.

Because of the dips in St Bernard's Road, remnants of the old gravel pits, the road invariably flooded in winter. At the Moulders' Arms a long piece of slate was put into slots near the entrance to prevent water running down the steps into the pub. Here is the present owner (taken in 1997), Mr Devand Mahabir, with his dog Sam, seated by the slate which he has just slotted into position, just as the publicans did in times gone by.

The Gardeners' Arms, 39 Plantation Road, was erected in the late 1830s. Richard Symonds recalls that for some years 'eminent literary characters associated with the Oxford University Press, such as Dan Davin, sat comfortably amongst aspiring writers who bought them drinks, though some of the latter got lost on the way, diverted to the other Gardener's Arms in North Parade.' Also, Mrs Shirley Ardener remembers that for many years, particularly in the 1980s, this pub was patronised by a group of well-known anthropologists who included Godfrey and Peter Lienhardt. It is said that Bill Clinton, President of the U.S.A. visted this pub when he lodged at 45 Leckford Road nearby.

The Anchor, 2 Hayfield Road, on the corner of Polstead Road. The original inn was established in 1796 on the site of Heyfield's Hut, kept by a Mr Heyfield who died in 1778. By 1845 it was called The Anchor because it was opposite the end of the canal and patronised by barge and boat people. In their account of Hayfield Road (1993) Catherine Robinson and Elspeth Buxton tell of a game of cards which took place when the eminent Dr Webb, 'tooth-drawer, blood-letter and wig-maker', lost 44 guineas and the mortgage deeds to two houses, probably to card-sharpers. In 1851 William Dolley, with his wife Charlotte, became landlord and the inn was nicknamed Dolly's Hut. They were there for 26 years and some of the local people still call it by this name. The picture shows how the pub looked before it was pulled down in 1936. (Photograph courtesy of The Anchor).

The Anchor in 1998 with its entrance in Polstead Road.

The Victoria at 90 Walton Street was built in 1839 and was owned for many years by Hall's Brewery. On the corner of the west end of St Bernard's Road, where the entrance now is, it has variegated brick and a mansard roof. At different times it was the headquarters of anglers, writers, poets, and Rugby players and was also at one time (unofficially) patronised by anthropolgists. Banks' Brewery chain took it over in 1995 and refurbished it to a high standard. Photograph taken in 1998.

# *People*

Katie Lucy in 1894.    One of Katie's sisters, probably Edith, in 1894.

The Lucys lived at 107 Woodstock Road. They owned and ran Lucy's Ironworks in Walton Well Road. (Both photographs courtesy of Christina Colvin).

Arthur Smith and family taken in about 1910. Back row, left to right: Alfred William (1899–1972), Ernest James (Dick) (1893–1915), (Albert) Percy (1895–1983), Arthur Edward Le Fevre (1889–?). Front row: Joyce (1892–1918), Arthur (1862–1944), Edith Mary (1890–1964). (Courtesy of Mr John Smith and Mr Colin Harris.)

The tailor. (Albert) Percy Smith (1895–1983) at work at Hall Brothers, Tailors, in the High Street, Oxford, where he was for 40 years. After his marriage he and his wife lived at 37 Plantation Road which had been his parents' and grand-parents' home since 1876. They later moved to 81 Plantation Road where they remained for the rest of their lives. (Courtesy of Mr Colin Harris).

Wedding of (Albert) Percy Smith, tailor, at the church of St Philip and St James to Gladys May Parsons on 7th June 1924. The small boy is Lawrence or Lovell Collier and the man on the right is (Ernest) George Clapton, baker, of Minster Lovell, later to become Gladys's brother-in-law. Gladys was born at 29 Plantation Road in 1899. (Courtesy of Mr Colin Harris.)

A 1913 reference given for the young James Walter Holt hoping to take on a pub in Reading. Brucker's establishment is where garages are now in St Bernard's Road (formerly St John's Road). Their garage was at No. 8. James Holt died in 1926 at the age of 55. He was for 21 years in the Royal Berks Regiment and served right through the First World War. He was a chorister at St John's College for the last seven years of his life. (Letter courtesy of Mrs Paula Simms).

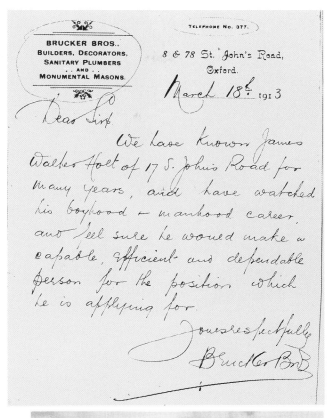

Number 2 Polstead Road taken in 1998. A plaque on the frontage records that it was where T.E. Lawrence ('Lawrence of Arabia') lived between 1896 and 1925. Thomas Edward Lawrence (1888–1935) was eight years old when he came to Oxford with his parents and brothers to live in this house. Here the family led 'a genteel life in the heartland of fashionable North Oxford, an area favoured by the middle and upper classes' (V.M. Thompson, 1990). T.E. went to the Oxford High School.

T.E. Lawrence, known as 'Ned' (left), when he was at Jesus College. He is seen here with his brothers (left to right) Frank, Arnold, Bob and Will.

The cottage in the garden of 2 Polstead Road where T.E. Lawrence worked when he was at Oxford University. Although No. 2 was semi-detached with No. 4, it was four storeys high and included a basement. Nevertheless, the cottage was built in 1908 so that Lawrence could carry on his University studies in relative peace and quiet. He had won a scholarship to Jesus College. There was a telephone extension fitted between the cottage and the house. The cottage/bungalow was later enlarged on the right-hand side and the garden shed in front of it is a recent addition.

Lawrence won a first-class degree in 1910 and was appointed a Research Fellow at All Souls in 1919. He recorded his Arabian exploits in *The Seven Pillars of Wisdom* which Jan Morris records was first printed by the Alden Press, Oxford 'with infinite care'. Lawrence changed his name to T.E. Shaw in 1927.

William Abraham Soden, chimney sweep, who lived at 73 Hayfield Road. He is shown still in his First World War Army breeches. (Photograph courtesy of Mr Richard Soden).

Sweeps had plenty of work in North Oxford with most of the houses burning fires in grates and chimneys requiring regular attention.

A recent Soden Sweep trade card.

2, JERICHO ST., OXFORD,

January 187'

Poultry Office

To ELIZA SODEN & SON,

LICENSED

Chimney Sweepers, Carpet Beaters, &c.

Soot supplied in any quantities, warranted free from adulteration.

POST CARDS AND LETTERS PROMPTLY ATTENDED TO.

A Soden billhead of 1891.

George Septimus Payne (1850–1933) and his wife Octavia (née Cundell) (1853–1937) (seated front right) after the wedding of their daughter Phyllis to Harry Critchley on 11th August 1909. The other guests are members of the Payne and Critchley families. (Photograph courtesy of Mr Peter Payne).

George Septimus Payne and his wife Octavia on the occasion of their Golden Wedding on 30th May 1928 together with four of their seven children and spouses. (Photograph courtesy of Mr Peter Payne). They are seated in the garden of 106 Woodstock Road where they lived from about 1924/25 when the house was built for them. Previously to this they had lived at 32 St Margaret's Road.

George Septimus Payne was a key figure in the long-established firm of Payne & Son, the gold and silversmiths and jewellers. Over the years the firm has had shops at Wallingford, Abingdon, Banbury and Tunbridge Wells as well as Oxford. George Septimus joined the firm in 1871 and in 1888 he bought the jewellery business of Alderman Sheard at 131 High Street, Oxford, where the Payne business still thrives today. He made it into a flourishing specialist silversmiths. Two of his sons and a son-in-law and daughter-in-law became directors of the Oxford firm as did two grandsons and a great nephew. As a great grandaughter and her husband also became directors of the Oxford establishment, now known as Payne & Son (Goldsmiths) Ltd., the family connections with it extend to four generations.

Back row, left to right: Janet M. Payne, Phyllis and Harry Critchley, Doris M. Payne, George Edward Payne (seated on right edge of bench) husband of Doris. Front: Muriel and Ewart Payne (seated on left end of bench), George Septimus Payne, Octavia C. Payne.

Octavia Payne outside 106 Woodstock Road in about 1930. It was demolished for the Trinity College annexe in 1978/9. Janet, the daughter of George Septimus and Octavia, lived there after the death of her parents until about 1968. She was a hospital almoner both in Oxford and in Australia. When she was in the latter country during the Second World War she let the house to the Moylan family. (See Section 2.) Photograph courtesy of Mr John Critchley. For further information see *Payne & Son. Two Centuries of a Family Firm,* by Judy and Stuart Dewey, 1990.

A Wedding Group after the ceremony in St Philip and St James Church, 9th April 1928. Back row, left to right: Christopher Carlton Clapton, Ivy Clapton (probably), William John Parsons (1873–1949), plumber, who lived in Plantation Road with his wife Minnie (née Holder) whom he had married in the same church in 1897. His father William, plumber and decorator, and mother Violetta (née Cross) also lived in Plantation Road. Between the two families they variously occupied Nos. 19, 35, 37 and 4l. Front row: (Ernest) George Clapton (groom), Marjorie Clapton Parsons (the bride), born at 29 Plantation Road. The little girl is not identified. The bride and groom started their married life in Minster Lovell but moved to 18 Kingston Road in about 1935 where they remained for the rest of their married life.

(Albert) Percy Smith and Gladys May Parsons photographed some time in the 1920s. After their marriage they lived with her parents at 37 Plantation Road and then moved in about 1933 to 83 Plantation Road where they lived for the rest of their lives. (Photographs courtesy of Mr Colin Harris).

Audrey Mary Smith, born at 37 Plantation Road, was given this Coronation souvenir with her photograph on it. She was eight at the time. In March 1949 she married Hubert George Harris, bookbinder at the Oxford University Press, at St Philip and St James Church. They began their married life at 83 Plantation Road before moving to Marston. Her brother John still lives at this house which means that the Parsons and Smiths families have been living in this road for 122 years. (Courtesy of Mr Colin Harris).

Miss Rosemary Spooner, the second daughter of the Reverend Dr William Archibald Spooner, lived at 9 Polstead Road with her double first cousin, Miss Ruth Spooner, from 1930 to 1969 when they left Oxford to live in Hampshire. Ruth was the daughter of Max, Dr Spooner's brother, and of Mrs Spooner's sister.

The two Misses Spooner became well-known Oxford figures, bicycling up and down Oxford's hills. They were both prominent in the field of social service and both accomplished musicians, Ruth at the piano and Rosemary on the cello. Rosemary also sang in the Bach Choir. These were, however, leisure pursuits for her because she spent much of her life in Oxford in public work. From 1946 to 1950 she was an Independent Councillor for the Summertown and Wolvercote Ward on Oxford City Council (at which time this photograph was taken) and she played a prominent part in the organisation of most of the Oxford hospitals. She was also Secretary of the Oxford Diocesan Council for the Deaf. Educational establishments, such as Ruskin College and the Oxford High School for Girls (whose governing body she chaired) benefitted from her support. She chaired various committtees in a most capable and friendly fashion. She died in February 1976 at the age of 89. Her father, the famous Dr Spooner, was Warden of New College from 1903 to 1924, after which the Spooners went to live at 1, Canterbury Road. He died in 1930. Rosemary said that the question of Spoonerisms was never mentioned in the family. Nevertheless the word has entered our language. On one occasion, recalls a friend, Rosemary suffered a slip of the tongue and blurted out: 'Oh, I nearly said one of those things!'

Mrs Paula Simms outside 17 St Bernard's Road with her son 'Skipper' (James John) in his basket seat taken in about 1945. Her grandparents, Mr and Mrs James Taylor Holt, lived in this same house and she and her father were both born there. When the St John's College 99-year lease ended, Paula's parents paid £1 a month rent to St John's. The house was pulled down and replaced by the St John's development of Arthur Garrard Close, named for the Bursar of St. John's (from 1949 to 1967). (Photograph courtesy of Mrs P. Simms.).

PUNCH AND BEVERIDGE

Lord Beveridge (1878–1963) lived for some years after his retirement at Staverton House, 104 Woodstock Road which University College had bought in 1953 and converted into flats, one of which was rented to Beveridge from May that year. The Beveridge Plan became the blueprint for welfare-state legislation from 1944 to 1948. He was not only Master of University College (1937–1944) but an Honorary Fellow of two other colleges. This cartoon, illustrating his resemblance to Mr Punch, was drawn by Chiang Yee in his book *The Silent Traveller in Oxford* (published by Methuen in 1944). He explained about the drawing: 'The upward curve of his wide mouth gave his face the effect of a permanent smile. Mr Punch is always smiling and thousands of people smile back at him. To a Chinese – a foreigner like me – Sir William and Mr Punch are both representative of England.'

Number 45 Leckford Road, Oxford (right) where William Jefferson (Bill) Clinton, President of the United States of America from 1993, lodged when he was a Rhodes Scholar at Oxford University. He was at University College where he is now an Hon. Fellow. He received a D.C.L. by Diploma in 1994. The photograph was taken in 1998.

Bill Clinton, President of the USA, seen here with his wife Hillary on the occasion of their visit to University College, Oxford in June 1994, after receiving his D.C.L. In the centre is the Master of the College, Professor W.J. Albery, D. Phil., FRS. (Photograph reproduced by kind permission of the Master and Fellows of University College.)

The proprietor of 'Daily Information' (established in 1963), Mr John Rose, with (left) Dan Butt and Pongus Lurcock. Taken in January 1998 in their premises in Warnborough Road. It is a hive of activity, not only publishing a regular 'Daily Information' sheet but is a bureau providing photocopying and computer services.

Nicolas Vernicoa (right) with his son Manos, partners in Bunters and the Post Office at 4 Hayfield Road since 1985. They are liked and admired by residents in the area. (Photograph taken in 1998.)